nd of liberty,   Of thee I sing;

ide,   From every mountain side   Let freedom ring.

Our Country's Story

OUR COUNTRY'S STORY

By FRANCES CAVANAH

Pictures by JANICE HOLLAND

RAND McNALLY & COMPANY • Publishers
New York · CHICAGO · San Francisco

AUTHOR'S ACKNOWLEDGMENT

OUR COUNTRY'S STORY is for boys and girls with little or no previous knowledge of history. It is hoped that this book will lead to the reading of other books, which will tell in more detail the wonderful, exciting story of the United States.

Writing a brief history for young children presents many problems. The author is grateful to the editors of Rand McNally & Company for their many helpful suggestions, especially to Marion Dittman, the editor with whom she worked most closely. Miss Dittman's unfailing kindness and understanding of each problem that arose helped to make OUR COUNTRY'S STORY possible.

The author also is indebted to William T. Hutchinson, of the Department of History, University of Chicago, who reviewed the manuscript for accuracy. To Janice Holland, the artist whose lovely, moving illustrations have made the book a thing of beauty, she can only say a very humble "Thank you."

F. C.

To Linda and Billy Lewis

Contents

Columbus Finds America 11

People Come Here To Live 13

The Pilgrims Have the First Thanksgiving . . . 16

The Dutch Buy an Island 19

William Penn Makes Friends with the Indians . . 20

The Colonies Get Better Acquainted 22

Paul Revere Gives a Warning 26

July 4 Is America's Birthday 29

George Washington Wins Our Freedom 30

Daniel Boone Crosses the Mountains 32

Lewis and Clark Go Exploring 36

"The Star-Spangled Banner" Becomes Our Song . 38

Boats and Trains Take People Places 40

Machines Make Work Easier 44

Pioneers Go West in Covered Wagons 47

Abraham Lincoln Keeps the Country Together . 50

The United States Reaches from Ocean to Ocean 54-55

The First Railroad Crosses America 56

Cowboys Ride in the Wild West 58

More and More People Come to America 60

Wonderful Things Happen 62

Airplanes Fly through the Sky 66

America Fights for Freedom 68

People Learn To Live Together 70

★ ★ ★

*These are only a few of the wonderful things that have
happened in our country. The story of the United States
is one that you will wish to go on reading in many books.*

Our Country's Story

Columbus FINDS AMERICA

Long, long ago a sailor named Christopher Columbus lived in Europe. He wanted to find an easy way of traveling to the Indies, the rich lands east of Europe.

"The world is round like an orange," he said. "We can reach the EAST by sailing WEST across the Atlantic Ocean."

Many people laughed at Columbus. But Queen Isabella of Spain gave him money to fit out three small ships. Columbus and his men sailed west for days and days.

"We can't see land any more," the sailors cried. "We're afraid. Turn back, Columbus, or we'll throw you overboard."

"We shall sail on," Columbus said.

At last they landed on a beautiful green island. It was part of the land we call America. But Columbus thought he had reached the Indies. When some red-skinned people came down to the shore, he gave them presents. Then, as the birds sang, the sailors knelt and kissed the ground. They were so happy to be on land again.

1492

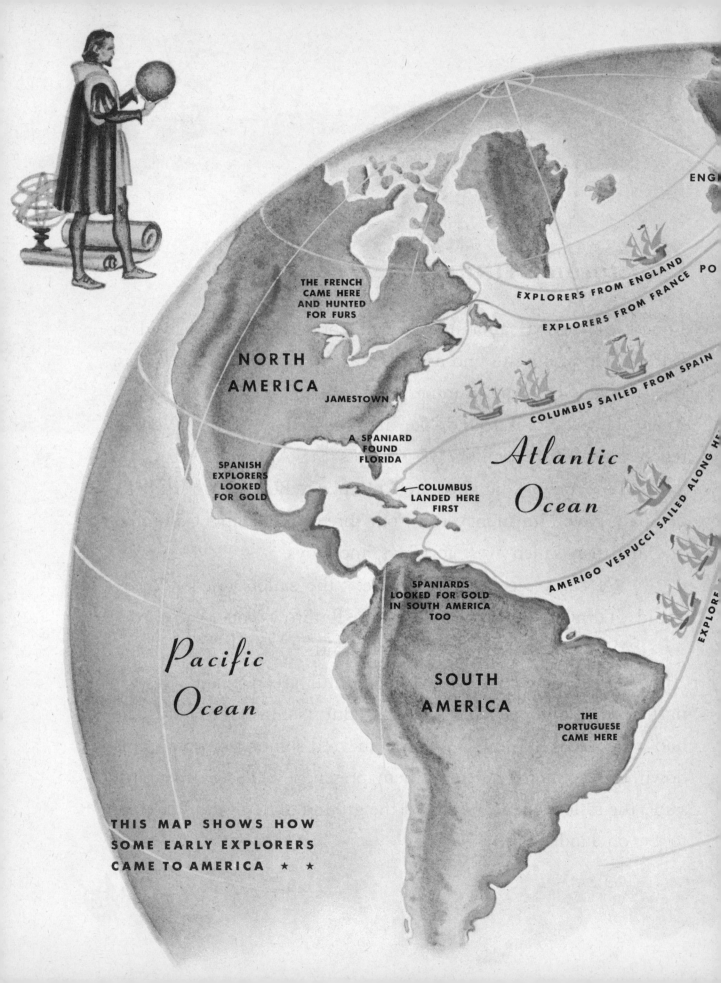

EUROPE

AFRICA

People Come Here TO LIVE

After Columbus other brave men, called explorers, sailed west to see what they could find.

"These new lands are not part of the Indies after all," said one explorer. "We have found a new world." This explorer's first name was Amerigo. So the new lands were called America. But the red men were called Indians, the name Columbus had given them.

Most of the explorers wanted to find gold and jewels. Then some Englishmen crossed the ocean to start a new colony, or home, in that part of America called Virginia.

"Maybe we'll find gold, too," said one colonist, "and so many jewels we can pick them up like pebbles."

But the colonists found no gold or jewels. They grumbled about this as they chopped down trees to build houses. They

grumbled about how hungry they were. The Indians who lived near by would not sell them any food.

"I'll *make* the Indians sell us some corn," said Captain John Smith, leader of the colony. "Then we must plant our own corn. We must fish and build traps to catch game to eat."

"But we are gentlemen," said some of the colonists. "We are not used to working with our hands."

"Well, if you won't work, you shan't eat," said Captain Smith. Then most of the colonists got busy. They had a hard time. Some months they almost starved. But they loved their new home and kept on working. Soon other English people came to Virginia to live.

That first little settlement was called Jamestown. It was the beginning of the United States.

14

The Pilgrims sailed across the ocean from England in a tiny ship, the "Mayflower," to start another colony. "The king wants everyone to go to the same church," they said. "But we want to worship God in our own way."

They landed in New England and built a town called Plymouth. During the first long, cold winter they were sick and hungry. But when spring came, everyone felt better.

One day a band of Indians visited Plymouth. "Red men want to be friends," they said. "Help white men fish, hunt, plant corn."

1621

IRST THANKSGIVING

Next fall the Pilgrims had plenty to eat from their gardens. They invited the Indians to a big dinner. A minister said a prayer: "We thank thee, Lord, for all thy blessings. We thank thee most for the freedom we have found in this new land to worship thee."

"Amen," said the Pilgrim children.

Then they looked up at the tables loaded with turkeys roasted crispy brown, golden ears of corn, and wild red berries. This was the first Thanksgiving dinner in America. They ate so much they forgot that they were ever hungry.

The Dutch BUY AN ISLAND

Several years later some Dutch colonists bought the island of Manhattan from the Indians.

"We'll pay for it with these bright beads, shiny knives, and beautiful red cloth," they said.

These things had cost only about $24.00, but at that time Manhattan was not worth much money. The Indians' eyes sparkled.

"Ugh! We sell," they grunted.

The Dutch built houses with steep roofs, like the houses in which they had lived in Holland. Red and yellow tulips bloomed in every yard. As the children played in the crooked streets, their shoes went clatter-clatter on the cobblestones.

Some of the Dutch fathers bought furs from the Indians. The furs were loaded on ships and carried across the ocean to be sold in Holland. Then the ships came back, bringing dishes and furniture and new clothes for the colonists.

The Dutch called their little town New Amsterdam. Later the English changed the name to New York. It became the biggest city in America.

William Penn

MAKES FRIENDS WITH THE INDIANS

Several other new colonies were started in America. And more and more people kept coming here to live.

Over in England there was a rich man named William Penn. He belonged to the church of the Friends, or Quakers. "The Friends are badly treated," he said, "because they do not worship God in the king's way. I shall start another colony in America, where they and everyone else can live in peace."

The king gave Penn a piece of land almost as big as England. It was called Pennsylvania. The trees were turning red and gold when Penn arrived in the fall with a band of colonists. They

20

began to lay out a town with wide streets and room for a garden around every house.

"We shall name it Philadelphia," said Penn, "because that means 'the city of brotherly love.'"

In some of the earlier colonies the Indians had tried to drive the white man away. There had been fierce fights between white men and red men. Many people had been killed.

But William Penn made friends with the Indians. He visited their villages. They had big feasts, and they played games.

"We are brothers," he told them. "God is the father of us all. He wants us to love and help and do good to one another."

The Indians liked William Penn. They knew he meant what he said. "We shall live in peace," they promised him, "as long as the moon and the stars shall shine."

The Colonies GE

After a while there were thirteen colonies in America.

In the South, tobacco and rice were grown on big farms called plantations. Some people became rich and lived in beautiful houses, with Negro slaves to work for them. Girls learned to dance and do fine sewing. The boys went hunting.

There were fine, big houses in the North, too. But most of the people lived in smaller houses. Girls learned to cook over a big open fireplace in the kitchen. The boys helped to make sugar for the family. In the early spring, when snow still covered the ground, they bored holes in the maple trees. The sap inside the

trees went *drip-drip-drip* into buckets. The mothers then boiled the sap in big kettles to make sirup and maple sugar.

"Yum-yum!" said the children, as they waited for a chance to lick the spoon. The sirup tasted just like candy.

In Boston and other New England towns many shipbuilders lived. Their ships, with big white sails, carried tobacco, lumber, and grain to be sold in cities along the coast or across the ocean. Many of the sailors on these ships visited far-off places.

But most of the colonists never traveled very far from home. Unless they lived near the water, almost the only way they

could travel was by horseback over rough, muddy roads. So people in the different colonies did not know one another very well at first.

Then after a while better roads were made. Bright-colored stagecoaches, drawn by horses, made regular trips between towns as trains and busses do today.

Tara-tara-tara! the stage driver would blow his horn. "Isn't it wonderful to travel at eight miles an hour?" said the passengers.

Benjamin Franklin, of Philadelphia, helped the colonists to know one another better. As postmaster of all the colonies he worked out ways to send mail faster. He hired men whom he knew he could trust to carry the mail on horseback. They rode

24

both night and day. It had once taken six weeks for a letter to go from Philadelphia to Boston, but now it took only six days. People in the different colonies wrote to one another oftener.

In his newspaper, the *Pennsylvania Gazette*, Franklin told the people of Philadelphia what was happening in other places. Newspapers were printed in other towns, and the readers learned what was going on in colonies besides their own.

"Why, we're all neighbors in America," some of the people said. Then they began to call themselves Americans.

Paul Revere GIVES A WARNING

Many of the colonists had come to America because they wanted to be free. Then the English king tried to make them obey some laws they thought were unfair. He sent his red-coated soldiers to Boston to make the people do as he said.

"We want to make our own laws," said the Americans. "We won't let soldiers from across the ocean tell us what to do. We'll fight the Redcoats if they aren't careful."

Young men, and older ones, too, practiced marching and shooting. They were called Minutemen because they promised to fight at a minute's notice. They hid some guns in the town of Concord near Boston, but someone told the Redcoats.

"We'll go out there and get the guns," the Redcoats said.

Paul Revere heard about this plan. He jumped on his horse and galloped out into the country. "The Redcoats are coming!" he shouted at every house he passed. "Be ready to fight."

When the Redcoats came the next morning, the Minutemen were waiting. The Redcoats fired. The Minutemen fired. They kept firing, firing, as they drove the Redcoats back to Boston.

July 4 IS AMERICA'S BIRTHDAY

When other Americans heard what had happened, they grabbed their guns and hurried toward Boston. They wanted to fight for freedom, too. In Philadelphia some men from the different colonies met in the State House.

"Let's ask George Washington to take charge of the new army," they said. "He used to fight the Indians. He was very brave when the red men tried to kill the white settlers."

George Washington, a tall farmer from Virginia, stood up. "I'll do my best to drive the Redcoats off," he said.

The next year Thomas Jefferson, another brave man from Virginia, wrote the Declaration of Independence. This said that all men are born free and equal. It also said that the colonies were now a nation called the United States.

On the Fourth of July the men in the State House voted to accept the Declaration. Several days later they told the people what had been done. *Ding-Dong! Ding-Dong!* The bell we call the Liberty Bell began to ring.

"Three cheers for the United States!" cried the people waiting outside. They never forgot our nation's first birthday.

George Washington WINS OUR FREEDOM

The Declaration of Independence *said* the colonies were free. But General Washington and his little army had to *make* them free.

The third winter of the war against the Redcoats the American soldiers camped at Valley Forge, near Philadelphia. They sat, shivering, around their campfires as the cold wind blew across the hills. Some of them were barefoot. They did not have enough to eat.

"The Americans haven't a chance against the Redcoats," many people said. But General Washington never gave up hope.

One day he had good news. Benjamin Franklin had gone to France to see the French king. The king had promised to send soldiers across the ocean to help drive away the Redcoats.

"Hurrah!" shouted the ragged soldiers at Valley Forge.

Every day they marched and drilled. By spring they were ready to fight harder than ever.

They went on fighting for several years. The Redcoats beat Washington in battle after battle, but he always came back to

fight again. At last the Americans, with the help of the French, surrounded the Redcoats at Yorktown, Virginia. The Redcoats had to promise to go home, and the war was over.

"We are free," the Americans cried. "We have our own nation now, because General Washington would not give up."

They called him the father of his country. Later they asked him to be the first president of the new United States.

Daniel Boone CROSSES THE MOUNTAINS

Most of the first colonists in America lived in the level land along the Atlantic Ocean. Only a few brave hunters ever climbed the mountains that lay to the west. One of the bravest of these was Daniel Boone. When he came home, he talked about the wonderful Indian country of Kentucky.

"There is free land out yonder for everyone," he told his neighbors. "I aim to go back and take my family."

Several other families wanted to go with Daniel Boone. They packed their things on horses for the long, hard climb across the mountains. Daniel Boone led them on and on until they came to the Kentucky River.

"I reckon you're the first little white girl who ever saw that river," he told his daughter, Jemima.

Daniel Boone's friends were called pioneers because they had come to a strange land. They named their new home Fort Boonesboro, after him. They lived in log houses inside a high log fence. Near by they started farms and planted orchards.

One day some Indians captured Daniel Boone while he was out hunting. They led him through the woods to their camp.

"We not want white people here," he heard them say. "This Indian land. We kill white people in fort."

As soon as he had a chance, Daniel Boone ran away. He hurried back to Boonesboro to warn the pioneers. When the Indians came, the men were waiting behind the log walls of the fort. They shot through the loop holes in the walls until the Indians went away.

The pioneers had to fight the Indians many times. But more and more people kept coming to Kentucky. Thousands of other people went beyond Kentucky to live in the wide valleys as far west as the Mississippi River.

At night, when the day's work was done, pioneer families would gather around the fire. "Pa, tell us a story about Daniel Boone," the children begged. The pioneers never forgot the brave hunter who had crossed the mountains. He had opened up a land where few white people had ever lived before.

Lewis and Clark GO EXPLORING

Suddenly the United States was twice as big as it had been before. President Jefferson bought from the French a big piece of land west of the Mississippi. It was called Louisiana.

"I want you to lead some explorers into the new country," he ordered his friends, Lewis and Clark.

The explorers rowed up the Missouri River. Lewis and Clark made maps of the country as they went along. During the winter they camped near the village of some friendly Indians.

36

"You cross Shining Mountains?" asked Sacajawea, an Indian woman. "I live there as a child. I show you the way."

In the spring the explorers started out again. Sacajawea went with them, carrying her Indian baby on her back. When at last they came to the steep, rocky mountains, she showed them the way across.

"Now we go on and on," she said. "Find Big Water."

Lewis and Clark passed through a rich, fertile land later called Oregon. At last they reached the blue Pacific Ocean. Then they went back home, and told about the wonderful Far West.

The Star-Spangled

While our explorers were going west, our ships were sailing east. They carried food and cotton to Europe. Then officers on English ships began stopping American ships to look for English sailors who had run away. Sometimes they took American sailors off the ships and made them fight in the English Navy.

The American people were angry. There was a quarrel which led to the War of 1812. Two years after it began, some English ships attacked the American

Banner BECOMES OUR SONG

fort near Baltimore, Maryland. Francis Scott Key, a prisoner on a ship near by, looked at the flag waving above the fort.

"What a beautiful flag it is," he thought, "with its broad stripes and bright stars."

Boom-boom-boom! All that night the guns roared. Mr. Key was afraid that the fort had been captured. But when morning came, he saw the flag still flying. He was so happy that he made up a song. He wrote the words on the back of an envelope:

"And the star-spangled banner in triumph shall wave,

O'er the land of the free and the home of the brave."

When Mr. Key went back to Baltimore, his song was printed. Soon people began to sing "The Star-Spangled Banner." Americans still sing it, for it is now our national anthem.

The year after Mr. Key wrote his song, the war was over. Ever since then the United States and England have been friends.

Boats and Trains TAKE PEOPLE PLACES

A little boat, the "Clermont," was moving up the Hudson River. "Look, it hasn't any oars!" said some people who were watching from the river bank.

"What makes the boat go?"

"It's a steamboat," one man replied. "It has an engine which uses steam to make the boat move over the water."

Robert Fulton, the inventor of the "Clermont," was on board the boat as it puffed its way upstream. It made the 150-mile trip from New York to Albany, without using either oars or sails. Soon other steamboats began making regular trips up and down the Hudson.

In a few years there were steamboats on other rivers in America. They carried people west to live.

But many people wanted to go where there were no rivers.

"They could travel on boats if we had a canal," said DeWitt Clinton, governor of New York. "Let's build one."

It took workmen eight years to dig the big ditch called the Erie Canal. When it was filled with water, it was like a river. It joined the Hudson River with Lake Erie, one of the Great Lakes inside America. Thousands of people who wanted to live near the Great Lakes traveled west on the brightly painted canal boats. Mules, walking on the bank, dragged the boats slowly through the water. The children played games on deck,

while their fathers talked and smoked. The mothers sat and knitted.

A canal trip was fun. Then people found a way of traveling they liked even better. In England a locomotive, another kind of steam engine, was invented. It was used to pull a train of cars. The train ran on rails, which were held together by crossties.

Soon there were railroads in America, too. The first engine to pull a train in New York State was called the "DeWitt Clinton," after the governor.

Toot-toot! The captain, or conductor, of the train blew a whistle when it was time to start. *Chug-chug-chug!* The train raced down the rails at nearly seventeen miles an hour. Smoke poured from the tall smokestack. Women raised umbrellas to keep off the flying sparks. B-U-M-P! The train stopped so suddenly that all the passengers were thrown to the floor.

Later, trains were easier to ride in. More railroads were built. After a while people could travel by train all the way from the Atlantic Ocean to the Mississippi River.

Machines MA

There was a time in America when most work was done by hand. Then machines were invented that made the work much easier.

Eli Whitney made a cotton gin to pick the seeds out of cotton. After that Southern farmers raised more cotton. They sent it to big buildings called factories. Workers in the factories used other machines to make the cotton into thread and then into cloth. A mother could now buy cotton cloth, instead of weaving it at home.

Then Elias Howe invented the sewing machine. *W-h-i-r-r!*

ORK EASIER

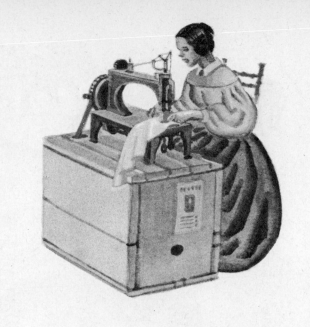

How much easier it was after that to sew the family's clothes!

The McCormick reaper was invented to help the farmer cut his wheat. He could now cut a big field in a few hours.

The most exciting invention was Samuel Morse's telegraph. A man sat at a machine, tapping out a message. *Dash-dot-dash-dot!* The dots and dashes stood for letters of the alphabet. Electricity carried the sounds over a wire to another machine. Longer and longer telegraph lines were built, and people hundreds and hundreds of miles apart sent messages back and forth.

Pioneers GO WEST
IN COVERED WAGONS

More and more pioneers went west to live. Some of them went to Texas, others to Oregon. Anyone willing to work hard could own a farm out west.

When gold was found in California, people all over the country were excited.

"Let's go to California and get rich," they said. "The gold is in the ground. All we have to do is dig it up."

Most of the pioneers rode west in big covered wagons or on horseback. Several families went together, so they could help one another. At night the wagons were drawn up in a circle. Camp fires were lighted, and the women cooked supper. Afterward someone might play a banjo while the others sang:

> "O California! That's the land for me,
> I'm going to California, the gold dust for to see."

When bedtime came, the people and animals slept inside the circle of wagons. The men took turns keeping watch.

West of the Mississippi they traveled across plains and

mountains. This was a wild land where only Indians lived. The Indians did not want the white people coming into this country. They attacked the wagons whenever they had a chance.

Often the guard saw dark figures creeping along the ground. "Indians!" he shouted. "The Indians are coming."

The pioneers grabbed their guns. Shot after shot rang out until the red men were driven off.

Many white people were killed in these attacks. Others were caught in snow storms when they crossed the mountains. But the pioneers went on and on until they came to California.

Taking their picks and shovels, many of the men began digging in the ground for gold. Some of them became rich. Others found no gold at all. But they found something much better—a rich, beautiful land of tall trees and fruit and flowers.

Many of the pioneers decided to stay in California.

Abraham Lincoln

KEEPS THE COUNTRY TOGETHER

The North and the South had a quarrel about slavery. Many Southerners owned Negro slaves. Many people in the North thought that the slaves should be set free.

"We are good to our slaves," the Southerners said. "We need them to work in our big cotton and tobacco fields."

Then Abraham Lincoln was elected President. He was a plain, homely man but wise and kind. He thought that slavery was wrong.

"Hurrah for honest Abe!" cried the people in the North.

But the people in the South were disappointed. They formed a new country called The Confederate States of America. Mr. Lincoln said that they had no right to do this. General Washington's soldiers had not fought and died for two little countries. They had wanted one strong, big country.

50

After Abraham Lincoln went to Washington to live in the
White House, the North and South made war on each other.
People on both sides thought that they were right. President
Lincoln was very sad when he heard about the terrible battles
that were being fought. His greatest comfort was his son, Tad.

Nearly every afternoon they walked across the White House lawn to the War Department to hear the latest news.

On New Year's Day, the third year of the war, the President signed an important paper which gave thousands of slaves their freedom. "Free at last! Free at last! Glory, glory, hallelujah!" the happy Negroes sang.

The war went on and on. The North had more soldiers than the South. The Northern soldiers had warmer clothes. Many of the Southern soldiers were in rags. They did not have enough to eat. But they kept on fighting for their brave general, Robert E. Lee.

At last he knew that they could not hold out much longer. He rode his horse Traveller over to see U. S. Grant, the Northern general. "My army is ready to give up," said General Lee.

The soldiers on both sides could now go home to their families. President Lincoln was very happy. All the states were together again in one country. The North and the South would be friends once more.

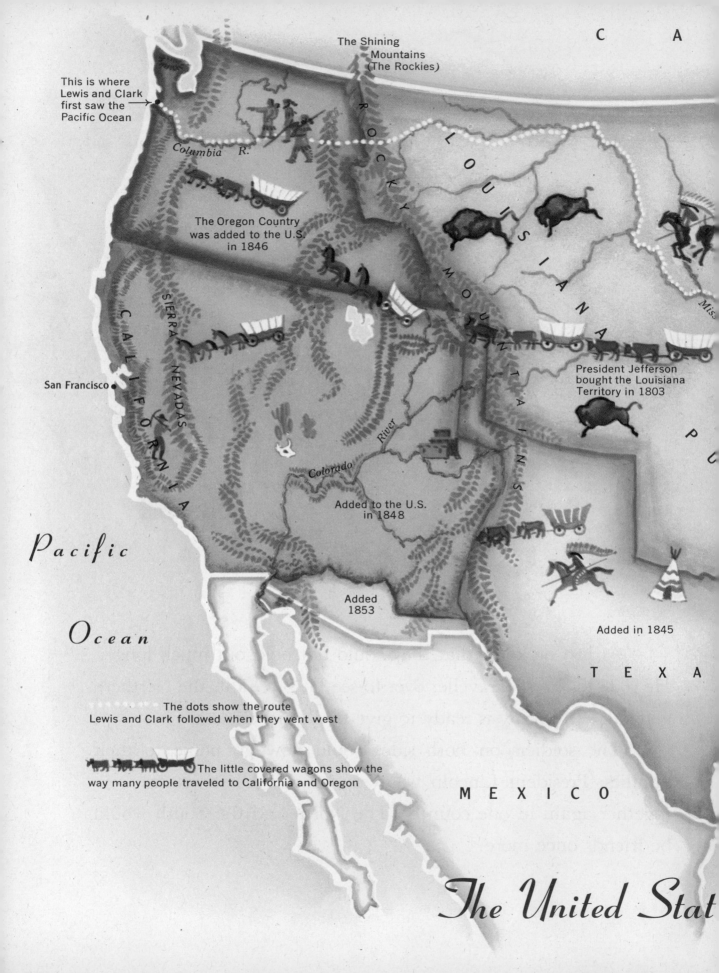

This is where Lewis and Clark first saw the Pacific Ocean

The Shining Mountains (The Rockies)

C A

Columbia R.

LOUISIANA

The Oregon Country was added to the U.S. in 1846

ROCKY MOUNTAINS

SIERRA NEVADAS

C A L I F O R N I A

San Francisco

President Jefferson bought the Louisiana Territory in 1803

Colorado River

Added to the U.S. in 1848

Pacific

Ocean

Added 1853

Added in 1845

T E X A

The dots show the route Lewis and Clark followed when they went west

The little covered wagons show the way many people traveled to California and Oregon

M E X I C O

The United Stat

A D A

Lake Superior

Lake Michigan

Lake Huron

Lake Ontario

Erie Canal

Lake Erie

Mississippi River

NEW YORK

N. H.

Boston

MASS.

Plymouth

R. I.

CONN.

New York

NEW JERSEY

PENNSYLVANIA

Philadelphia

Baltimore

M A R Y L A N D

DELAWARE

Washington

VIRGINIA

Hudson R.

M T S.

These were the Thirteen Original Colonies

Lewis and Clark started here

St. Louis

Ohio River

Boonesboro

The U.S. reached to the Mississippi River in 1783

A P P A L A C H I A N

NORTH CAROLINA

SOUTH CAROLINA

GEORGIA

Atlantic

Ocean

Mississippi River

New Orleans

F L O R I D A

Added 1821

Gulf of Mexico

...ACHES FROM OCEAN TO OCEAN

The First Railroad

Even while the North and the South were fighting, new settlers were going west. They traveled as far as they could by railroad, then usually rode in stagecoaches the rest of the long way.

"It takes nearly a month to cross the country," people grumbled. "We need trains that will go farther west."

At last it was decided to build a railroad all the way to the Pacific. Workers living in California started to lay tracks eastward across the mountains. Other workers, starting in the new state of Nebraska, laid tracks westward.

ROSSES AMERICA

One-two-three-four-five-six years went by. Then one bright May day the two bands of workers met near Ogden, Utah. The last rails were laid. That afternoon, as a crowd of people watched, the last wooden crosstie was put in place. Down the tracks came two trains—one from the east, one from the west.

Closer, closer, they came, until the engines touched.

"Hurrah!" The crowd tossed their hats into the air.

All over the country people were happy. "Now we can travel from the Atlantic to the Pacific in a few days," they said.

Cowboys Rid

Many battles were fought between white men and red men in the West. But at last the Indians gave up. Our government sent them to live on big places called reservations.

Then cowboys came to live on the plains east of the Rocky Mountains. They drove herds of cattle up from Texas to graze on the tall grass. Each spring and fall they rounded up the calves.

THE WILD WEST

Twirl-twirl! A cowboy would twirl a long rope, making the end into a circle. The rope flew through the air. It landed around the calf's neck. Hundreds of calves were caught in this way.

" 'Whoo-pee! Git along, little dogies,' " the cowboys sang, as they drove the little calves up the trail to the rich grasslands in the North.

For a long time the land west of the Mississippi was called the Wild West. Robbers held up trains. Rustlers, or thieves, stole cattle. But at last most of the bad men were driven out. Cowboys looked after the cattle on big ranches. New pioneers came to the plains and started farms.

The Wild West had become tame.

More and More People

COME TO AMERICA

The United States is a land of many *immigrants,* people coming from another land. Even the Pilgrims were immigrants.

New immigrants kept coming, not only from England but from other countries. After the war between the North and the South, thousands sailed into New York harbor every year. Most of them had been very poor in the Old World.

"In America," they said, "we can get a job or start a farm. We won't be afraid of cruel kings or unfair laws. Americans make their own laws. They can even vote for President."

Some of the immigrants helped to build new railroads. Many of them worked in factories and mines. Others went west to start new farms. They forgot that they had once been Irishmen or Swedes or Germans or Russians. They became Americans, and they helped to make our country strong.

When the United States was one hundred years old, the people of France decided to give the people of America a birthday present. This was the Statue of Liberty. For many years it has stood in New York harbor, to welcome those who come here from other lands.

Something very wonderful happened the year our country was a hundred years old. Alexander Graham Bell used electricity to carry the sound of a person's voice over wires. He called his invention the telephone. Soon telephone wires were stretched from house to house and from city to city. People could talk with their friends in the next block or hundreds of miles away.

One of our country's greatest inventors was Thomas Edison. He was nicknamed the "Wizard," because he found so

Things HAPPEN

many new uses for electricity. He made an electric light to take the place of candles and lamps. With thousands of electric lights shining in the dark, cities looked like fairyland at night. Mr. Edison also helped to give us movies. He was one of several inventors who worked on motion-picture cameras. He invented the phonograph, a machine that talked.

Dash-dot-dash-dot-dot! The inventor, Marconi, found a way to send telegraph sounds through the air without wires. Other in-

63

ventors learned to "broadcast" music and the sound of people talking. Their invention was called the radio. Children could listen in their own homes to an orchestra playing miles away. They could hear a man talk or sing on the other side of the world.

Even pictures were sent through the air. People with television sets could both hear and *see* a program.

For a long time inventors had tried to find better ways of traveling. The first automobiles were called "horseless carriages." Instead of being pulled by horses, they were run by electricity, steam, or gasoline. They chugged and bumped over the rough roads. But the owner of a horseless carriage felt very proud. "Just think," he boasted, "I can travel at fifteen miles an hour!"

After a while better roads were built. Better automobiles were made. People rode in swift, streamlined automobiles and in busses and trucks all over our big country. New streamlined trains sped across the United States. Fast, comfortable ocean liners carried more and more Americans each year across the oceans and around the world. Men, women, and children who lived thousands of miles apart began to get acquainted.

Much faster than the ocean liners were the airplanes. They were faster than the swiftest stream-lined trains. They flew through the air like giant birds, carrying mail and people.

For hundreds of years men had wanted to fly. At last two Americans, Orville and Wilbur Wright, built a flying machine.

Some of the people who saw it laughed. "It looks like a big box with wings," they said.

The Wright brothers took their new invention to a hillside in Kitty Hawk, North Carolina. It was a cold December day, and only five people came to watch them try it out. Orville climbed into the plane. He started the engine. The plane rose. It stayed in the air *twelve seconds*, then landed safely on the ground.

A way had been found for man to fly.

Thousands of bigger, better airplanes have been made since then. They fly across the United States. They fly on regular trips across the oceans. Today fast, shining planes soaring through the sky make every country in the world our neighbor.

America Fights FOR FREEDOM

American soldiers fought for freedom during World War I. The American people never wanted to go to war again. They thought that freedom was something they would always have.

But in some parts of the world millions of men, women, and children were not free. During World War II German and Japanese soldiers marched into one country after another. When a country was conquered, the people had to do whatever the soldiers told them. If they did not obey, they might be killed.

"We shall conquer the earth," the leaders of the soldiers bragged. "Everybody else in the world shall be our slaves."

Then the Americans knew that they would have to fight again for freedom. They fought hard—the soldiers, the sailors, the marines, and the men who flew the planes. At home men and women made guns and machines to help win the war. Boys and girls collected scrap and waste paper.

President Franklin Delano Roosevelt often talked over the radio to the people of America. "We are going to win this war," he said, "and we are going to win the peace that follows."

He meant that there must never be another war again.

People LEARN TO LIVE TOGETHER

The United States is strong because Americans have helped one another. The early colonists and pioneers worked together. Years later, when many men and women were out of work, American leaders helped them to find jobs.

"We have a rich country," people said. "We want everyone to have enough to eat, warm clothes to wear, and a nice

place to live. We can make this wish come true, if we all help one another."

American boys and girls learn to work and play together at school. Some of them are children of immigrants from Sweden, Russia, Italy, and other countries. Some of them are the great-great-great-grandchildren of the early colonists and pioneers.

Some of them are great-great-grandchildren of Negro slaves. But they all sing "The Star-Spangled Banner." They study the same lessons. They play tag and ball and hide and seek. They are learning to get along with one another so they can keep our country strong.

"Countries must learn to help one another, too," our people say. "Then we can keep the countries that want war from hurting the countries that want peace."

American boys and girls know they will always love America best, just as they love their own families best. But they want to be *friends* with all the other people in the world. They know that everybody, everywhere, will be happier when people learn to live in peace and friendship.

My country, 'tis of thee,   Sw

Land where my fathers died,   Land of the Pilgri